DANCING ON THE CEILING

inspired by
The Metamorphosis
by Franz Kafka

Austin Tichenor

BROADWAY PLAY PUBLISHING INC
New York
www.broadwayplaypublishing.com
info@broadwayplaypublishing.com

DANCING ON THE CEILING
© Copyright 2006 by Austin Tichenor

First printing: December 2006
I S B N: 978-0-88145-317-1

Book design: Marie Donovan
Word processing: Microsoft Word
Typographic controls: Ventura Publisher
Typeface: Palatino
Printed and bound in the U S A

DANCING ON THE CEILING was originally produced by the American Stage Festival Young Company in Milford, New Hampshire in August 1987. The cast and creative contributors were:

GREGOR .... Sarah Williams
FATHER .... Dee Ryan
MOTHER .... Mark Dold
GRETE .... Brian Jennings
BOSS .... Scott Pegg

Director .... Austin Tichenor
Costumes & scenery .... Jeff Boring
Lighting .... Kace Christian

A revived production (with revised script) toured New England in 1989. The cast and creative contributors were:

GREGOR .... Rosalyn Coleman
FATHER .... Lillian Dean
MOTHER .... Matthew Skwiot
GRETE .... Michael McAllister
BOSS .... Janet Lefkowitz

Director .... Dee Ryan
Costumes & scenery .... Jeff Boring
Lighting .... Kace Christian

CHARACTERS

GREGOR
GRETE
MR SAMSA (FATHER)
MRS SAMSA (MOTHER)
BOSS

Note: In order to shake up all questions of identity within the family, GREGOR *and his* FATHER *are played by women,* GRETE *and her* MOTHER *by men.* BOSS *can be cast either way, unless a third option becomes available, in which case go with that.*

A NOTE FROM THE AUTHOR

Kafka for kids? Is *that* a good idea? Fortunately, with a slight change in tone, it is. The story's fantastical elements strikes a chord with adolescents who are often experiencing their own struggles with changing bodies.

DANCING ON THE CEILING was conceived as an expressionistic fairy-tale about identity and role expectations, and the original designs reflected that. The scenery was at odd angles, the lighting was sharp and angular, and the costumes were basic pieces (apron, skirt, beer-belly T-shirt, etc) over a unisex outfit. Because this is a play about appearances, all the dressing and moving scenery was choreographed as part of the reality of the world and done in plain view.

Similarly, GREGOR's metamorphosis was achieved not through elaborate special effects or prosthetics but through sounds, lights, and the actors' own spectacular physicality. Each woman from the original two productions was a different kind of GREGOR, so each went through a different transformation. The trick seems to be illustrating for the audience that her body now has different parts (antennae, additional legs, etc.) and always struggling with what is now a very strange and cumbersome shape. Only when he dances on the ceiling should GREGOR achieve any kind of grace.

The Young Company solved the dance-on-the-ceiling challenge as described in the script. The broom that FATHER carries was attached to a fishing line so that when GREGOR threw it down [up] onto the floor, an offstage stagehand yanked the other end of the line and the broom went flying into the air and out of sight. If there's a way to fly the actors without making it too "Peter Pan", I envy your theater's facilities.

Music provides a rich texture of sound and can create GREGOR's odd world. Maybe it isn't "music", per se; maybe it's just sounds. One production in Boston created a score that set my words to original music.

So have fun with it! It's a fable that should be scary, funny, and hopefully moving. Try to honor the darkness while retaining the hope that GREGOR gains at the end.

And I urge you to adhere to the concept of reverse-sex casting. It underlines that this is a play about identity. Since GREGOR's transformation relies on the actor's skill over special effects, you're way ahead of the game with a woman playing GREGOR. Once the audience accepts at the outset a woman saying, "I'm just a normal boy", they'll accept anything.

(A funky odd song begins. A light rises on GREGOR, *dressed in shorts and shirt, maybe a baseball cap, over dyed surgical sweats.)*

(He stares straight ahead, then his head and shoulders twitch and turn sharply—up, right, left, right, ahead, left, left. He brings his armS around to the front of his body and we realize he's on a pitcher's mound, staring down his batter.)

*(*GREGOR *winds up and pitches—and the ball is knocked clean out of the park.* GREGOR *goes through his ritual again as lights come up behind him, revealing four other ball-playing kids.* GREGOR'*s clumsy and inept, and they tease him.)*

*(*GREGOR *sighs, picks up his books and heads home. The ball players come downstage and assume the garb of* GREGOR'*s family:* FATHER *puts on a beer-bellied t-shirt;* MOTHER *puts on curlers, an apron, and dishwashing gloves; and* GRETE *puts a skirt on and a bow in her hair.)*

*(*GREGOR *arrives home and finds his* FATHER *drinking a beer and reading his paper, his sister quietly folding laundry, and his* MOTHER *washing dishes.)*

*(*GREGOR *flops down, hoping for a rest, but his* MOTHER *comes over and dumps a basket of laundry over his head. He sits amid the pile of clothes as the music fades.)*

GREGOR: *(To the audience)* The weird thing is, I'm like everyone else. I'm just a normal boy. Just a normal boy living in a normal family. I've got one of everything: a father, a mother, and a sister. Perfectly normal.

FATHER: *(Looking up from his paper)* Gregor! What is that you're doing?

GREGOR: Mother asked me...

FATHER: Folding laundry is women's work, Gregor!
A boy like you should not be folding laundry.
There's a right way and a wrong way for a boy to
behave. You need to be tough, Gregor! People in this
world will take advantage of you unless you are strong.
They will squash you like a bug!

GREGOR: *(To the audience)* He just wants what's best for
me. Life any father.

(MOTHER hustles over to take over the laundry chores.)

MOTHER: Oh honey, you're absolutely...I shouldn't
have...It's my, it's all my...Here, let me take this,
you shouldn't—Grete! Why aren't you folding your
brother's...what is *this*? Gregor! Haven't I asked you
to wipe your feet when...you're leaving little tracks,
little footprints all over the...never mind, I'll...
(As she goes) Honey, can I get you another—?

GREGOR: *(To the audience)* She works so hard. Always
making sure we're happy. Just like every mother.
And my sister—

(He crosses to her; she's folding laundry.)

GREGOR: She's so quiet. Like she's not even there.
I watch out for her. That's my job...well, it's one of
my jobs.

*(FATHER leaps up and begins pacing. MOTHER re-enters and
tries to calm him.)*

FATHER: *(As he paces)* Money money money money
money money money money money money money
money money money money money money money
money money money money money money money

money money money money money money money money money money money money money money money...

MOTHER: *(As she paces)* Dollars and cents, and dollars and cents, and dollars and cents, and dollars and cents, and dollars and cents, and dollars and cents, and dollars and cents, and dollars and cents, and dollars and cents, and dollars and cents ...

GREGOR: *(As they pace and chant)* My father got fired from his job—well, *gets* fired from his job. A lot. He has one and then he doesn't....or wouldn't...or can't...or won't. And my mother's real busy taking care of us. So I have a job! I go to it every day. I bet I work harder than any kid I know! *(Realizing)* Yeah. I bet I do!

(Lights up on BOSS *atop a tall ladder, wearing a white coat and tie over his surgical sweats.)*

BOSS: *(Leaning down from on high)* Gregor!

GREGOR: Yes, sir?

BOSS: You're late, boy! You should have been here ten minutes ago!

GREGOR: Yes, sir. I'm sorry, sir. My teacher asked me to stay after school and—

BOSS: I'm not interested in your excuses, Gregor. Being sorry doesn't get the job done!

GREGOR: Yes, sir!

BOSS: And you're getting sloppy, too. I'm watching you, Samsa, like I watch all you leeches. Be careful—I know how to deal with blood-sucking parasites like you!

GREGOR: Yes, sir. *(To the audience)* A boss really has to be pretty strict. *(Then)* So every day I go to work, go to school, go to work, go home, go to bed; go to work, go to school, go to work, go home, go to bed. Except on weekends, when I go to work, *stay* at work, go home, go to bed; go to work, *stay* at work, go home, go to bed.

(The other four form a human assembly line, gesturing mechanically and repeating the litany.)

ALL: *(Except* GREGOR*)* Go to work, go to school, go to work, go home, go to bed; go to work, go to school, go to work, go home, go to bed. Go to work, *stay* at work, go home, go to bed; go to work, *stay* at work, go home, go to bed.

GREGOR: That's it. That's what I do. Just like every boy. And at night, before bed, I like to relax in the warmth of my family.

FATHER: *(Stepping off assembly line)* Gregor!

GREGOR: Yes, Father!

FATHER: How long have you been working at the factory?

GREGOR: Um, a couple of years.

FATHER: You deserve a raise.

(The assembly line stops.)

FATHER: Tomorrow, I want you to ask your boss for a raise.

(The line breaks up and moves away.)

GREGOR: Tomorrow? But Father, just today my boss...

FATHER: What? What did your boss? Are you in trouble?

GREGOR: No Father, it's just I don't think I can...

FATHER: Good. Then tomorrow you can ask him for a raise.

GREGOR: You think I should?

FATHER: I said so, didn't I? You need a raise. We need the money.

GREGOR: All right, Father, if you think...

MOTHER: Gregor, honey, would you like—?

GREGOR: A glass of milk? Yes, please. *(To the audience)* I *love* milk.

(GRETE enters with a tray of food items.)

FATHER: Grete! What are you doing?

GRETE: I'm cleaning out the refrigerator. Mother asked me to.

MOTHER: Yes, honey, I asked her—

FATHER: But what is that?

GRETE: It's just some mouldy old cheese and rotten vegetables. I'm throwing them out.

FATHER: *Doonn't* throw those out!! We are not so wealthy that we can afford to throw out perfectly good food!

MOTHER: Honey, your father's right, I didn't mean—

GRETE: But Mother, it's rotten!

MOTHER: Oh dear, honey, she's right, it's all—

FATHER: We cannot *afford* to let food spoil!

GRETE: But who will eat it?

MOTHER: *(Helpfully)* Don't worry, dear, your father will eat it.

(MOTHER hands the rotten food to her husband. FATHER looks at the food in his hands.)

FATHER: Uhh...here, Gregor. You eat it. Be good for you.

(He hands the food to GREGOR, *who struggles with it, unsure of what to do.* MOTHER *and* GRETE *turn away, unable to help.*

FATHER: Oh, never mind, Grete! Just put it back. Do as I say!

*(*GRETE *bursts into tears.* MOTHER *comforts her, while at the same time trying to explain to her husband.)*

MOTHER: Oh now, honey, don't cry, he didn't mean to...honey, she didn't mean to...he was just trying to explain how we've...she was just doing what she thought I told...I'm sorry, honey, it's my fault, I shouldn't have told you to...I'm sorry, honey, it's my fault, I shouldn't have told her to...shh, shh...

*(*GRETE'*s tears have by now become sniffles.)*

MOTHER: Shh, honey...shh...Remember this old...
(She sings a verse or two of this nursery rhyme.)
Ten little soldiers
Marching in a line
One fell out of step
And then there were nine

Nine little soldiers
Marching through a gate
One tried to go around
Then there were eight

Eight little soldiers
Marching through the sticks
Two stopped to look around
Then there were six

Six little soldiers
Marching home alive
One tried to run ahead
Then there were five

Five little soldiers
Marching home from war
One stopped to smell a rose
Then there were four

Four little soldiers
Marching through debris
One tried to clean it up
Then there were three

Three little soldiers
Marching past a view
One began admiring it
Then there were two

Two little soldiers
Marching towards the sun
One found a shady spot
Then there was one

One little soldier
Made it on his own
Finally he looked around
And saw he was alone
(She keeps singing quietly.)

GREGOR: *(To the audience)* Pretty normal. I'm going
to bed. Since I get up early, I go to bed early. *(He goes
into his bedroom and climbs onto his bed, It's an oddly
proportioned parallelogram, the head of which is higher than
the foot. To the audience)* Sometimes, if Mother isn't busy,
she has time to come tuck me in.

*(MOTHER comes into the room. Music begins,
accompaniment to the nursery rhyme.)*

MOTHER: Six little soldiers
Marching home alive
One tried to run ahead
Then there were five
(During the second verse, however, something changes.)

Five little snoldarts
Marching louse from wee

GREGOR: What? What was that?

MOTHER: One lorched a snose to flau
Fie nerva fee

GREGOR: Wait. What did she say?

MOTHER: Good night, Gregor. Rarble kupke.

GREGOR: What? Mother, what did you say?

MOTHER: I said, good night, Gregor. Pleasant dreams.

GREGOR: Oh. That's what I thought you said.

(MOTHER *leaves. To the audience:*)

GREGOR: That's not what I thought she said. I thought
she said... marble cupcake, or something. Boy, I must
be tired. (*He gets out of bed, goes over to the door, locks it,
then gets back into bed.*) At night, before I go to bed. I can
finally—relax. (*He "relaxes": his body remains stiff and
rigid.*)

GREGOR: At night, I don't have to be a worker. Or a
helper. Or a protector. Or a soldier. I can be who I am.
(*Thinking*) Whoever that is. (*He falls back on his bed, fluffs
his pillow, tries to get comfortable in a variety of positions,
but can't.*) Come on, Gregor—you had a busy day
today, and you have a busy day tomorrow. And a busy
day the day after that. And after that. And after that.
So get to sleep! (*He tries different, strange positions, but
they don't work either. He sits up in frustration.*) Come on!
Oh—I don't feel very well. I feel kind of—funny...

(*There's a burst of electronic sound.* GREGOR *twitches.*

GREGOR: What's going on? What's happening?

(*Another electronic burst. He twitches again.*)

GREGOR: Hey, stop it. My body's doing really weird—

(But GREGOR *can't talk any more because his body is changing. His arms and legs get skinnier—and multiply. His back becomes rounder and harder, armored. Antennae sprout from his head. His entire body becomes wider. Still standing, he tries to walk on his new legs, but his old sense of balance won't work with his new body, and he falls over on his back onto the bed. He tries to get back onto his feet but can't.)*

GREGOR: Oh no. What is this? *(He tries to get up.)* Unh! I can't get up. What am I? It looks like I've turned into some sort of—giant cockroach! Ugh. Come on, get up. Get—*up! (But he can't. Calling:)* Mother! Help me! Mother! Fa—wait a second! I can't call them in here. They'll be terrified! Unless— *(Thinking)* Unless...I wonder, maybe this is something that happens to *every* boy! Maybe it's just a *phase! (Beat)* But I need to get up. I need to get up and go to work. Help! Mother! Father!

*(*FATHER *and* MOTHER *stumble sleepily up to* GREGOR'*s door.)*

FATHER: *(Knocking)* Harfa! Roo la tigger? *[Gregor! Are you all right?]*

MOTHER: *(Also knocking)* Harfa! Tas a siyon? *[Gregor? What was that noise?]*

*(*GREGOR'*s startled: the sounds he hears coming out of his parents' mouths are indecipherable gibberish.)*

GREGOR: What? Why are they talking like that? Mother! Father! Help me! I can't get up!

*(*GREGOR'*s parents are startled, too: instead of* GREGOR'*s voice, all they hear are the grunting of a large animal.)*

MOTHER: On nee! Ra dial lamina ray a Harfa! *[Oh no! There's a wild animal in there with Gregor!]*

FATHER: *(Pounding on the door)* Harfa! Frillik, neepo sith rood! *[Gregor! Goddammit, open this door!]*

MOTHER: Harfa! *[Gregor!]*

(Note: The transcription of the gibberish is for clarity. The important thing is the action being played, not the "words" being said.)

GREGOR: I don't know what they're saying. I'm going to be late for work! *(Calling) Don't worry, I'm all right! This is probably just one of those twenty-four hour things.*

(GRETE has woken up from all the noise and stumbles in.)

GRETE: Tas neegoy? *[What's going on?]*

GREGOR: That's Grete. She sounds all funny, too!

MOTHER: On Hempa! Dial lamina neetay Harfa! *[Oh Grete! A wild animal has eaten Gregor!]*

GRETE: Tas! Roo nod? *[What? Are you sure?]*

GREGOR: I can't understand any of them! *(Realizing)* I bet the whole family has turned into bugs!

(FATHER has produced a ring of keys and tries to unlock the door.)

FATHER: Frillik, chew yeek sit... *[Goddammit, which key is it...]*

GREGOR: Come on, Gregor, get up! You should have been at work minutes ago!

(BOSS suddenly appears. He speaks gibberish as well. GREGOR keeps trying to right himself.)

BOSS: Essuke sem, ring la tigger? *[Excuse me, is everything all right?]*

MOTHER: Nee, dial lamina neetay Harfa! *[No, a wild animal has eaten Gregor!]*

FATHER: *(Kissing up to the boss)* Wann, nee wonk roo nod. Nath koo king reer. Ee nod Harfa kees. *[Now, we don't know that for sure. Thank you for coming here. I'm sure Gregor's just sick.]*

BOSS: Lew, Harfa tile krow *nen*, ee sideeded mock reer. *[Well, since Gregor was late for work **again**, I decided to come over.]*

FATHER: On, syu, *syu*, nath koo, nath koo, roff king reer! *[Oh, yes, yes, thank you, thank you for coming here.]*

BOSS: *(Knocking on the door)* Harfa! Sith sobb! Roo la tigger! *[Gregor! This is your employer. Are you all right?]*

GREGOR: My boss! I can't let him see me like this! This may be normal, but it's real embarrassing.

BOSS: *(Pounding now)* Harfa! Nee rom mages! Neepo sith rood! *[Gregor! No more games! Open this door!]*

(Finally, GREGOR *manages to right himself.)*

GREGOR: There! Oh—it's so hard to walk!

FATHER: Harfa! Ro sobb sine a king reer...Neepo sith rood! *(To* BOSS*)* Mi reeso, rise, nee wonk a Harfa sith rorn. Harfa stum kees. Nee wonk sigh k'tah nee sine... *[Gregor! Your boss was nice enough to come here...open this door! (To* BOSS*) I'm sorry, sir, I don't know what's with Gregor this morning. He must be sick. I can't think why he would act in this inconsiderate...]*

(Meanwhile, GREGOR *has found his feet and started to scrabble across the room. He speaks as he moves, and as he clumsily tries to open the door.)*

GREGOR: I'm sorry, sir, you must believe that I would never be this late for work unless there was a very good reason. You see, I take my employment at your store very seriously, not only because I need the money, that is to say, my *family* needs the money, but because I know you to be an honest and fair man...

(But as GREGOR *begins talking, the others become still, listening to the growlings and gruntings from the creature in the next room. As* GREGOR *nears the door, the others back away, not knowing what they're about to see.)*

GREGOR: ...and I know how terribly lucky I am to be able to work at your fine establishment. I beg you to forgive my tardiness this morning not for me, because I'm really not worth it, but for my parents, who have struggled long and hard to provide for me and my sister, and they deserve the consideration. Please sir, won't you find it in your heart to forgive me?

(On his last two words, GREGOR *flings the door open.)*

(Beat)

(The others react. MOTHER *screams and holds onto* GRETE, *who doesn't appear to be affected at all.* FATHER *stands between the two Samsa ladies and the monster.* BOSS *remains paralyzed. Mouth-open and wide-eyed, he stares at this...thing.* GREGOR *steps closer to him.)*

GREGOR: You see? I'm not feeling at all like myself...

*(*BOSS *screams and runs out the front door. Both* GREGOR *and his* FATHER *start after the* BOSS *to stop him, but run into each other at the door. They freeze, staring at each other until* GREGOR *makes the first move.)*

GREGOR: *(Reaching out)* Father?

*(*FATHER—*seeing and hearing only a large cockroach— yells and backs away from* GREGOR, *and runs off through a different door.)*

*(*GREGOR *turns to his* MOTHER *and* GRETE. MOTHER *babbles hysterically [in gibberish] as* GREGOR *moves closer to them.* MOTHER *grabs* GRETE's *hand and starts to go, but* GRETE *slips through her grasp.* GREGOR's *now between* GRETE *and his* MOTHER, *who's too scared to move.)*

*(*GREGOR *and* GRETE *study each other carefully. He looks back and forth between* GRETE *and his* MOTHER, *then takes a stop towards* GRETE. GRETE *reaches a tentative hand out towards* GREGOR—*which is exactly when* FATHER *appears in the doorway brandishing a broom.)*

GRETE: Rothev, nee! *[Father, no!]*

(FATHER steps between them and smacks GREGOR solidly on the back with the broom. It makes a loud hollow wooden sound. GREGOR flinches away.)

FATHER: Teeg kabba! *[Get back!]*

(FATHER drives GREGOR back to the doorway of his room.)

GREGOR: *(Reaching out)* Father! Mother! Grete!

(But FATHER swings the broom again and GREGOR stumbles backwards into his room, shutting the door. FATHER locks the door, then backs away. GREGOR collapses and lies in an exhausted heap on the floor.)

(The lights change. Many hours later)

(GREGOR licks his wounds. In the other room, the Samsa family begin to attempt to figure out what has happened. They go to the door and try to look through the keyhole, while Gregor writhes on the floor in pain and reaches out his arms for help.)

(GRETE gets an idea. As FATHER and MOTHER are distracted, consoling each other, she gets a bowl of milk and quietly unlocks GREGOR's door. Steeling herself, she goes in.)

(GREGOR scuttles away from the door, warily watching GRETE approach. Staring at her brother, GRETE carefully puts the milk down on the floor, indicating that it's for him. Then she goes.)

(As soon as she's gone, GREGOR scrabbles over to the bowl and dips his head to drink—but immediately spits it out.)

GREGOR: Pthehh! That's horrible! What's the matter— I used to love milk. It must be spoiled. *(He sniffs at the milk, then tries it again. And spits it out again.)*

GREGOR: No, it's not spoiled, it's perfectly fresh. I just think it's horrible now. I didn't used to. What am I supposed to eat? *(Looking around)* I've been in here for *hours!* My sister is the only one who's tried to communicate with me all day. It was very nice of her to bring me the milk. I hope she's not upset that I didn't like it. Oh, I'm so hungry! *(Beat)* And I have to go to the bathroom.

(He hears a sound at the door and quickly scrabbles away from the bowl. GRETE *sticks her head in cautiously and enters. She goes over to the bowl and looks up in surprise.* GREGOR *shakes his head.)*

*(*GRETE *thinks a minute, then gets an idea. Indicating that* GREGOR *should wait, she picks up the bowl [with a cloth, not with her hands] and leaves the room.)*

*(*GREGOR *goes over to the keyhole, peers through it, then scuttles away as* GRETE *returns, this time carrying an assortment of food items. She lays them down in a row on the floor and backs out of the room.* GREGOR *goes to the food.)*

GREGOR: Let's see what she brought me this time. A bowl of water, some apples, some almonds, some raisins, some coffee cake, ugh! All that rotten food: rotten lettuce, that old cheese, ak—and an old bone with gristle on it. Let's see... *(He tries the water first. It's okay. The raisins, coffee cake, and raisins are unappealing— but the rotten lettuce, after some hesitation, proves to be* very *good. So does the mouldy cheese.)* I'll save this bone for later—and when this apple gets really brown and squishy, it'll be great!

*(*GRETE *comes back in unexpectedly and* GREGOR *scrabbles quickly away. She looks at the food and is pleased that he liked some of it. She begins to clear it away when* GREGOR *suddenly rushes over to her.)*

*(*GRETE *backs away but* GREGOR *only wants to hang on to the bone. He backs respectfully away, and* GRETE *finishes picking up the remnants of the food and leaves. Music begins, a haunting melody.)*

GREGOR: And so, for the last few weeks, that's how I've been taken care of. My sister comes in twice a day and brings me water and all the scraps she can find.

(GREGOR *scoots himself under his bed and* GRETE *comes in with a duster, bucket, and mop.*)

GREGOR: My little sister—the one I protected—now protects me. She cleans my room every day. (*Whispers*) She even cleans up my bathroom corner. (*Looking at her*) I know it must be hard for her to look at me, so I hide under the bed whenever she comes in. Even though we can't talk to each other, I like it when she comes in because I can watch her and she reminds me of what I used to be. (*Beat*) I haven't seen my mother and father at all. Oh, I've heard them. At night, I go to my door and listen. I can't tell what they're saying, but it's good to hear their voices.

(FATHER *is railing about something in the background, his* MOTHER *is trying to placate him, and* GRETE *looks from her* MOTHER *and* FATHER *to* GREGOR.)

GREGOR: My boss never came back. I bet I got fired. Perfectly normal—just like my dad. (*Beat*) I figured out that my family hasn't changed—yet. But what if it's contagious? What if I'm the first one to get it? What if the rest of my family is about to catch the disease?

(*Music changes: something appropriate for a* Cockroach Ballet. FATHER, *still railing, begins to twitch and change.* MOTHER *and* GRETE *suddenly begin to twitch and change, too. They all fall over onto their backs, but* GREGOR *helps them all right themselves.*)

(*Suddenly,* BOSS *appears in the doorway. He, too, has changed.* GREGOR *rallies the family to help him, and* GREGOR *climbs to the top of the Boss's ladder to preach to and lead the next generation of cockroaches.* GREGOR's *family and boss march off through the doorway to a brave new world, but* GREGOR *remains behind, his daydream over. Music fades.)*

GREGOR: What if this is *all* a dream? Maybe I'll wake up one day and I'll be a boy again. Oh, I hope so! But wait— *(Realizing)* Wait a minute! What if I've *always* been a bug? What if I'm a bug who's dreaming that he used to be a boy? Oh, don't let it be that!

(GRETE runs in, frightened. Somehow, she manages to communicate that something's up. She motions to GREGOR to come quietly to the door. FATHER and MOTHER enter. He's carrying a "House For Sale" sign.)

FATHER: Nee yenom! Nee *yenom!* *[We have no money! No money!]*

MOTHER: Bud a boo Harfa? *[But what about Gregor?]*

FATHER: Harfa rya ned! Harfa ray dial lamina! Nee rake a boo Harfa! Rake a boo sith mafily! *[Gregor is dead! Gregor is a wild animal! I don't care about Gregor! I care about this family!]*

MOTHER: Harfa ray sith mafily! *[Gregor is a part of this family!]*

FATHER: *Nee! Nee! Harfa nee* trop sith mafily! *[No! No! Gregor* is *a part of this family!]*

(GRETE pushes GREGOR back into the room and looks at him: what are we going to do?)

GREGOR: *(To the audience)* I don't know what they're saying, but I know they're talking about me. Harfa means me.

(GREGOR communicates physically with GRETE, and translates what both are saying.)

GREGOR: I have to leave? *(As GRETE)* "No, no, not you—we are leaving." *You* are leaving?

(GRETE nods her head. Yes.)

GREGOR: What about me?

(GRETE *shrugs and shakes her head. I don't know.*)

GREGOR: Oh no. *(To the audience)* Without me working at the factory, my family can't afford to live in this house. They're selling it for the money and moving! They can't do that! They can't leave me here! What'll become of me?

(GREGOR *scrabbles over to* GRETE *as music begins.* GRETE, *startled by the sudden movement, panics and runs out of the room.*)

(GREGOR *paces as* GRETE *pleads with her parents not to move.* FATHER *storms off and* MOTHER—*after hesitating between her daughter and her husband—runs off after* FATHER.)

(GRETE *returns to* GREGOR's *room and approaches him slowly. She reaches out and gently touches* GREGOR *for the first time.* GREGOR *flinches a little but doesn't run.*)

(GRETE *places her hand on her chest and points to* GREGOR. GREGOR *places his hand on his chest and points to* GRETE. *She gathers up her courage and takes* GREGOR's *hand and only flinches once.*)

(*Music fades as* FATHER *enters followed by* MOTHER *who's not placating anymore.*)

FATHER: Nee, nee, nee! *[No, no, no!]*

MOTHER: *(Demanding)* Syu, syu, syu! Manda ees Harfa! Manda ees mi noss! *[Yes, yes, yes! I demand to see Gregor! I demand to see my son!]*

FATHER: Say dab eeday... *[It's a bad idea...]*

(GRETE *motions for* GREGOR *to wait, and runs into the other room to help calm her* MOTHER *down.*)

MOTHER: Ooya nee kinth a boo Harfa! Tawan ees
Harfa! *[You don't want us to think about Gregor! I want to
see Gregor!]*

GRETE: Rothem, nee kinth ooya... *[Mother, I don't think
you...]*

MOTHER: Tawan ees Harfa! *[I want to see Gregor!]*

FATHER: Nee! Stissen nee ees Harfa! *[No! I insist you
cannot see Gregor!]*

MOTHER: NEE RAKE! *[I DON'T CARE!]*

(FATHER's *aghast at this outburst.* MOTHER's *pleasantly
surprised by her sudden show of strength.)*

FATHER: Ooya yas? *[What did you say?]*

MOTHER: Yas, nee rake! Tawan eese Harfa! *[I said,
I don't care! I want to see Gregor!]*

GRETE: Rothem... *[Mother...]*

MOTHER: Hempa, tawan ees Harfa. *[Grete, I want to see
Gregor.]*

GRETE: Wann? *[Now?]*

MOTHER: Tigger wann. Tawan ees mi nos. *[Right now.
I want to see my son.]*

FATHER: Sith dab eeday... *[This is a bad idea...]*

MOTHER: Shh! *[Shh!]*

(GRETE *takes her* MOTHER's *arm and leads her towards*
GREGOR's *room.* GREGOR *scrabbles away from the door,
looking for a place to hide. He finally gets himself under the
bed just as they appear at his door.)*

(MOTHER, *for all her determination, is still one frightened
lady. She reacts to the stench.* GRETE *tries to calm her,
assuring her it'll be all right.* MOTHER's *eyes search the
room, wondering where her son could be.)*

(GRETE *begins to sing the nursery rhyme.*)

GRETE: *(Singing)* Veef tillie snoldarts
Chumping louse a wee
Nuhwa lorched a snose to flau
Fie nerva fee

(Her MOTHER *nervously joins in.)*

MOTHER & SISTER: *(Singing)* Veef tillie snoldarts
Chumping louse a wee
Nuhwa lorched a snose to flau
Fie nerva fee

(GREGOR, *hearing the familiar tune, cautiously sticks his head out from under the bed.* MOTHER *sees his head and freezes.* GRETE *soothes her and motions for* GREGOR *to come out.)*

(GREGOR *slowly slides all the way out from under the bed and presents himself.* MOTHER *isn't breathing very well, but she's doing the best she can.)*

GRETE: Rothem, sith see Harfa. *[Mother, this is Gregor.]*

(MOTHER, *almost paralyzed, sticks her hand out but immediately withdraws it. She and* GREGOR *stare at each other.* GRETE *discreetly steps away;* MOTHER *doesn't like being left alone but stands her ground.)*

(GREGOR *touches his chest and points at his* MOTHER; *she doesn't understand.* GREGOR *repeats the move;* MOTHER *looks to* GRETE *for translation.)*

(*But instead of trying it a third time,* GREGOR *steps toward his* MOTHER—*and her nerve completely shatters. Screeching music begins.)*

(MOTHER *screams and runs out of the room.* GRETE *follows and leaves the door open. Without hesitation,* GREGOR *leaves his room and runs after them.)*

MOTHER: *(Seeing him)* Nee, mi reeso! Bekabba, bekabba! Mi reeso! *[No, I'm sorry! Get back, get back! I'm sorry!]*

(GREGOR, *helpless, keeps taking steps towards his* MOTHER, *wanting to help. His* MOTHER *runs to the other side of the room.* GREGOR *looks to his sister for help while his* MOTHER *continues to babble in gibberish.*)

GRETE: Harfa! Bekabba ray moor, Harfa. Rothem nee katey. [*Gregor! Go back to your room, Gregor. Mother can't take it.*]

(*Suddenly,* FATHER *appears, drawn by the commotion, holding his broom. He moves toward* GREGOR, *trying to herd him back into the room, but* GREGOR's *focused on trying to help his* MOTHER. FATHER *whacks* GREGOR *on the back with the broom. It makes the same loud hollow wooden sound.*)

(GREGOR *stumbles, and turns to face his* FATHER.)

FATHER: Tee kab! Tee *kab* roo moor! [*Get back! Get* back *in your room!*]

(GREGOR *looks to his sister.*)

GRETE: Syu, Harfa, seeple tee kab roo moor! [*Yes, Gregor, please get back in your room!*]

(GREGOR *looks at his* MOTHER, *whose back is toward him, whimpering. He takes a step towards her and* FATHER *whacks him again.*)

(GREGOR *stumbles, then wheels to face his* FATHER. *They stare at each other, daring the other to make the first move. Finally* GREGOR *turns to his* MOTHER *and his* FATHER *raises his broom—but* GREGOR *rears up and knocks the broom out of his* FATHER's *hands.*)

(FATHER *backs away, and now the combined sounds of* FATHER *ordering,* GRETE *yelling, and* MOTHER *crying and pleading start to get to* GREGOR. *Confused, hurt, unable to think, he looks at each of his family in turn, then emits a wild silent scream and claps his arms over his ears. All sound and music stops.*)

(GREGOR's silent scream continues. He looks at his family and removes his arms from his ears. The cacophony resumes. GREGOR covers his ears again and the sound stops, but as he runs back into his room, his arms drop and the horrible racket resumes.)

(Only when he slams his bedroom door do the noises mercifully cease.)

(GREGOR's family goes off. GREGOR paces: upset, scared—and angry.)

GREGOR: They don't like me! They think I'm a monster. I'm not, I'm just a...I don't know what I am. They don't want me because I'm not what I was. *(Thinks)* Well, what was I? I was just everybody's...little soldier! Well, I'm not! I'm a boy! Just a normal living... *(Realizing)* No, I'm not. I'm not normal at all!

(Music starts.)

GREGOR: I'm a bug! I'm nobody's little soldier anymore! I'm a great big not normal great big bug! And...I...can... do...*anything*!

(Wild celebratory music surges. GREGOR jumps onto his bed, looks at his arms and legs, then jumps onto the wall.)

(As GREGOR hits the "wall", stagehands or other actors turn the bed on its side and bring in a large upside down chandelier which they place center.)

(Then GREGOR jumps up [down] onto the ceiling and dances around the chandelier. He hangs by his arms, then by his legs. He's having the most fun he's ever ever had.)

(He dances on and on. At one point, drawn by the commotion, GRETE comes in—upside down. She's delighted by how much fun GREGOR's having.)

(But then FATHER comes in—also upside down—holding his broom. [Both actors are either held upside down, or hang

upside down with their knees hooked over actor people's shoulders.])

(GREGOR *waves to* GRETE *and his* FATHER *from the ceiling.* FATHER *pokes the broom up at him but can't quite reach.* GRETE *tries to get her* FATHER *to stop, but he pokes the broom up again. This time, Gregor grabs the broom and throws it down [up] into his bathroom corner.)*

(FATHER *leaves the room but* GRETE *wants to dance on the ceiling too. She reaches up and* GREGOR *takes her hand. They dance this way for awhile until* GRETE *dances off.)*

(GREGOR *keeps dancing, then jumps down onto the wall, then onto the floor [as the bed and chandelier restore to their original positions]. He looks up the ceiling and smiles. Music fades.)*

GREGOR: The body of a bug, the brain of a boy! Gregor, the Bug Boy! What should I do next? So many possibilities. *(He struts around, trying to decide.)*

GREGOR: I can wait. I'll start tomorrow. I'm exhausted!

(He gets into bed, pulls the sheet over him and prepares to go to sleep, but the change music begins again. He twitches.)

GREGOR: Oh no. What is this?

(Music again. GREGOR *twitches again.)*

GREGOR: Oh no, it's happening again! What am I gonna change into this time?

(GREGOR *twitches as his body changes. His many cockroach arms and legs spiral down to two of each, his back concaves back into human form, and his antennae pull back into his head. Gregor stands metamorphosed—back into a boy.)*

GREGOR: Look. Look! I'm a boy! I'm a boy again! I'm a...I'm a *naked* boy is what I am... *(He rushes to put on his shorts and shirt.)* Wait'll I tell them! Wait'll they see me! Wait'll...wait a second. What if *this* is a dream? What if I'm still a cockroach dreaming that he's turned back into the boy he used to be? Was *that* a dream? Is *this* a dream? *(Panicking)* Grete! Mother! Father!

(He runs into the other room and GRETE, *his* MOTHER, *and* FATHER *all run in to meet him.)*

GRETE: Gregor?

(And now, of course, they all speak in English.)

GREGOR: Grete, I'm back. I'm back, Mother.

(He embraces his MOTHER *and sister. His* FATHER *looks at him suspiciously, and checks his room to make sure that bug isn't still around here somewhere.)*

MOTHER: I'm so sorry for crying, honey, I just couldn't... I tried not to, because I knew that...but when I saw you...I mean, when I saw that hideous monst... No, I mean when I saw *you*, I just felt so helpless that I...you're my boy, you're my baby Gregor...

GREGOR: What? What did you call me?

MOTHER: Gregor. I said your name. Gregor.

GREGOR: It's nice to hear that name again. For a long time, I could only hear you calling me—

FATHER: Harfa! My boy, it's good to see.

*(*GREGOR *turns to his* FATHER.*)*

GREGOR: What did you say?

FATHER: I said it's good to see you, Gregor, my boy.

GREGOR: Oh. I thought you said...never mind.

MOTHER: Honey, we're so glad to see you.

FATHER: I knew you'd be back, Gregor. I knew you'd do the right thing. I knew you wouldn't let your family down.

GRETE: What was it like, Gregor? What did it feel like?

GREGOR: What did it feel like? It was... *(Searching for the right word)* Surprising. I saw things...differently. And I realized that a lot of things around here were really...bugging me.

FATHER: Come along, Gregor, we need to get you your job back.

(Beat)

GREGOR: No.

FATHER: What?

GREGOR: I said—

MOTHER: *(Strong)* No. Gregor is a boy again. And we are going to let him stay a boy until...well, until he changes again.

(FATHER glares at them and exits.)

MOTHER: Don't you worry about him. You be a boy, and I'll get him to for once start acting like a man!

(And she follows FATHER off.)

GRETE: He's still planning on moving to a smaller house.

GREGOR: Good. We don't need this big ol' place anyway.

GRETE: But how can we afford it? You can't get your old job back?

GREGOR: Hey, I've been a bug, I knocked a broom away from my father, and I danced up on the ceiling of my room. I can start all over again...and so can Father!

GRETE: Gregor, you sound different.

GREGOR: *(Surprised)* I do? I don't feel different. *(Laughs)* I'm just a normal boy, living in a normal family.

(The haunting music from before begins again.)

(GREGOR touches his hand to his chest and points to GRETE. She repeats the gesture back to him. They embrace as the lights fade.)

END OF PLAY

www.ingramcontent.com/pod-product-compliance
Lightning Source LLC
Chambersburg PA
CBHW070037110426
42741CB00035B/2804